PIANO Adventures® *by Nancy and Randall Faber*
THE BASIC PIANO METHOD

T0020136

CONTENTS

About the "Sightreading Stocking Stuffers"

A student's enthusiasm for learning Christmas music can become an opportunity to create enthusiasm for sightreading. In this book, each Christmas song is presented with short melodies, called "Sightreading Stocking Stuffers."

The "Sightreading Stocking Stuffers" are **melodic variations** of the carol being studied. Teachers will notice that the lyrics and rhythm patterns are from the carol. By drawing on these familiar rhythms, the student may effectively focus on interval reading and note reading.

The student should sightread one "stocking stuffer" a day while learning the Christmas song. Or, the stocking stuffers can be used as sightreading during the lesson itself.

The teacher may wish to tell the student:

> **Sightreading means "reading music at first sight."**
>
> When sightreading, music is not practiced over and over. Instead, it is only played once or twice with the highest concentration.

The following **3 C's** may help the student with sightreading:

 CORRECT HAND POSITION
Find the correct starting note for each hand.

 COUNT - OFF
Set a steady tempo by counting one "free" measure before starting to play.

 CONCENTRATE
Focus your eyes on the music, carefully reading the intervals.

FF1138

Stuffing the Stockings

Each musical "gift" is an interval: **2nd**, **3rd**, **4th**, or **5th**.

Draw a line connecting each "gift" to the correct stocking.

Extra Credit: Play each "gift" on the piano using the fingering given.

Angels We Have Heard on High

Traditional

Teacher Duet: (Student plays *1 octave higher*)

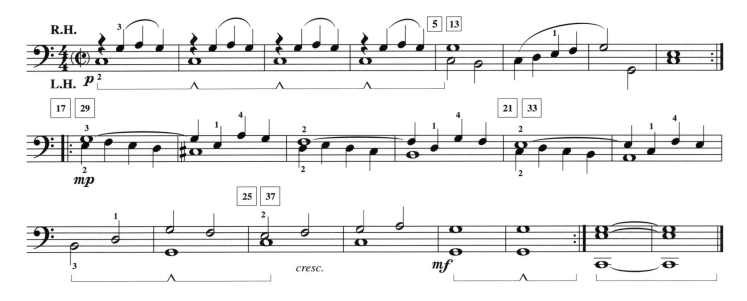

4   FF1138

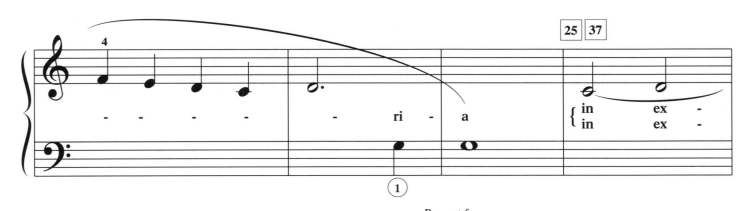

- - - - - ri - a { in ex -
in ex -

Repeat from measure 17.

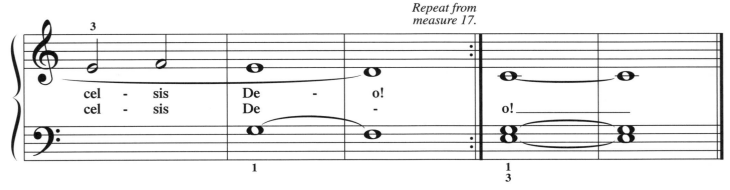

cel - sis De - o!
cel - sis De - o!

Sightread one "stocking stuffer" a day while you are learning the carol.
The words to the "stocking stuffers" are familiar, but the **melodies have changed!**

Circle the stocking after sightreading!

CHRISTMAS STOCKING STUFFERS

("variations" for sightreading)

DAY 1

1 *on* ____?

f (An - gels we have heard on high,)

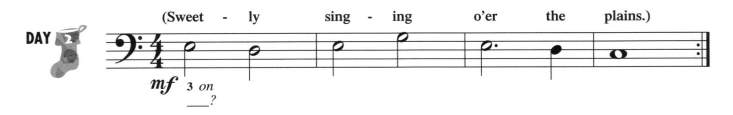

(Sweet - ly sing - ing o'er the plains.)

DAY 2

mf 3 *on* ____?

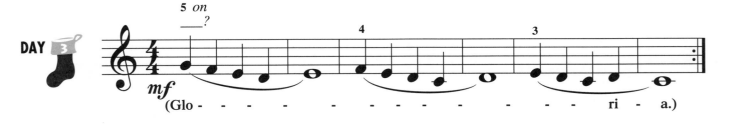

5 *on* ____?

DAY 3

mf
(Glo - - - - - - - - - - - ri - a.)

DAY 4 Can you find the melody of **Day 2** in the carol? Hint: It is in the treble clef.

DAY 5 Can you sing from measure 17 to the end of the carol?

Up on the Housetop

Words and Music by
Benjamin R. Hanby

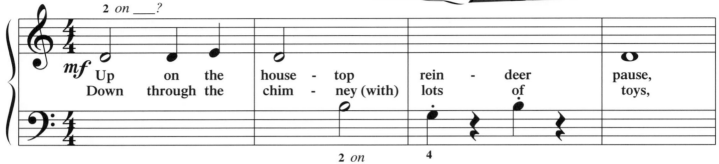

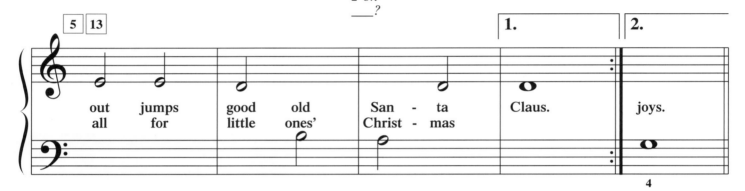

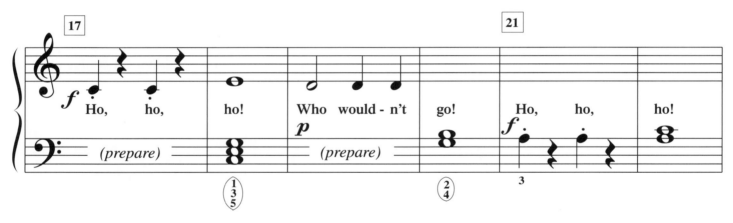

Teacher Duet: (Student plays *1 octave higher*)

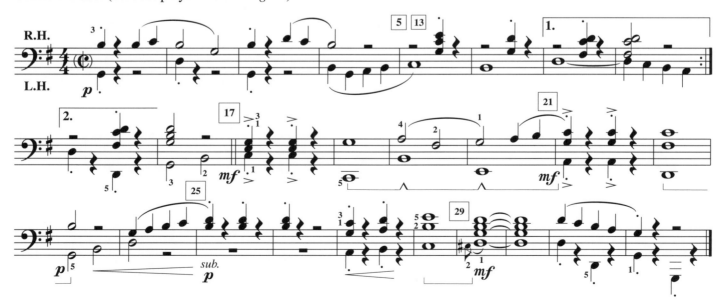

FF1138

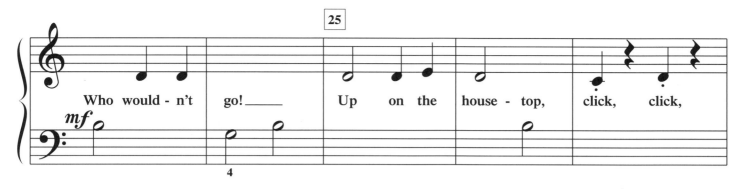

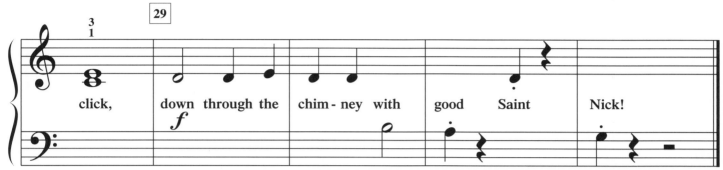

Sightread one "stocking stuffer" a day while learning *Up on the Housetop.*

Circle the stocking after sightreading!

("variations" for sightreading)

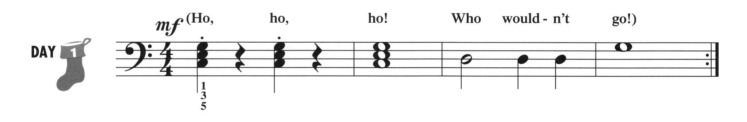

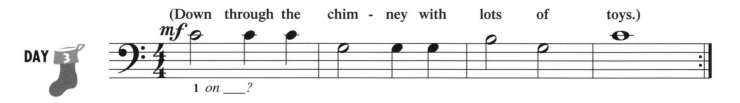

DAY 4 Circle all the **4ths** in the "stocking stuffers" above.

DAY 5 In *Up on the Housetop,* put a ✔ above each measure with this rhythm:

  Hint: There are 5 measures.

We Three Kings of Orient Are

Words and Music by
J.H. Hopkins, Jr.

Flowing smoothly

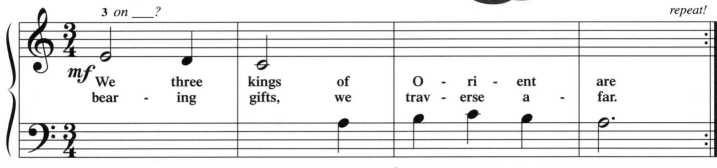

3 *on* ___?   *repeat!*

We three kings of O - ri - ent are
bear - ing gifts, we trav - erse a - far.

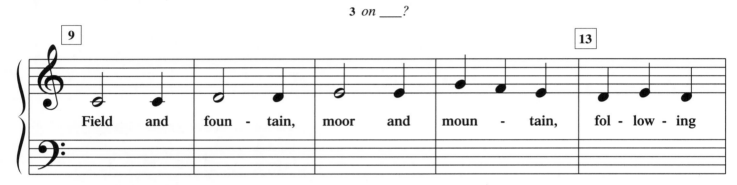

3 *on* ___?

Field and foun - tain, moor and moun - tain, fol - low - ing

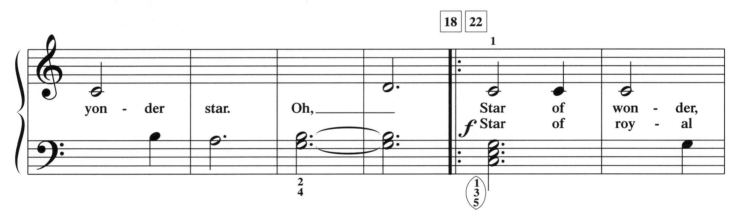

yon - der star. Oh,_____ Star of won - der,
Star of roy - al

Teacher Duet: (Student plays *1 octave higher*)

R.H.

L.H. *p*
with pedal

FF1138

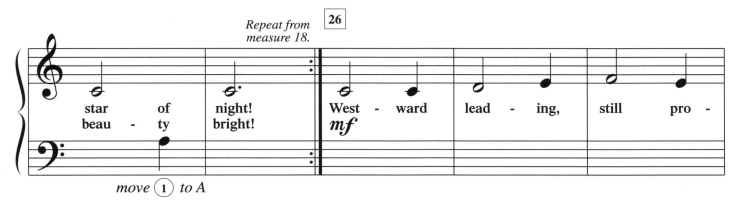

star — of — night! / beau — ty — bright! *mf* West — ward — lead — ing, — still — pro -

move ① to A

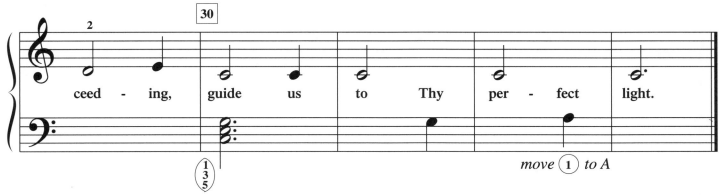

2 30

ceed — ing, — guide — us — to — Thy — per — fect — light.

move ① to A

Sightread one "stocking stuffer" a day while learning *We Three Kings of Orient Are.*

Circle the stocking after sightreading!

STARRY STOCKING STUFFERS

("variations" for sightreading)

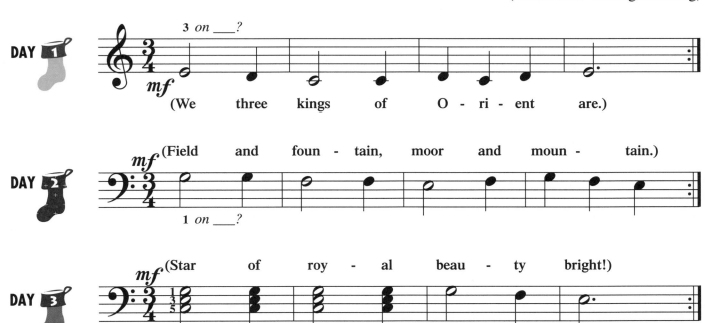

DAY 1

3 on ___?

mf

(We three kings of O - ri - ent are.)

DAY 2

mf (Field and foun - tain, moor and moun - tain.)

1 on ___?

DAY 3

mf (Star of roy - al beau - ty bright!)

1
3
5

1

DAY 4

Write the counts "1 - 2 - 3" under the beats for **Day 3.**

DAY 5

Circle the most common rhythm in *We Three Kings of Orient Are.*

♩ ♩ ♩ — or — ♩ ♩ ♩ — or — ♩.

Deck the Halls

Merrily

Traditional

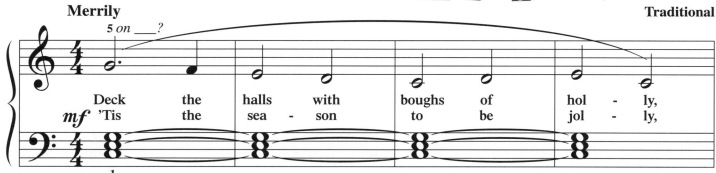

5 on ___?

Deck   the   halls   with   boughs   of   be   hol -   ly,

mf 'Tis   the   sea -   son   to   be   jol -   ly,

1
3
5

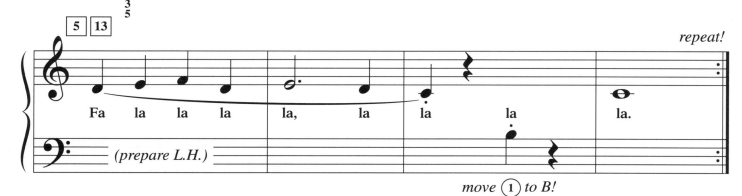

5 **13**

repeat!

Fa   la   la   la   la,   la   la   la   la.

(prepare L.H.)

move ① to B!

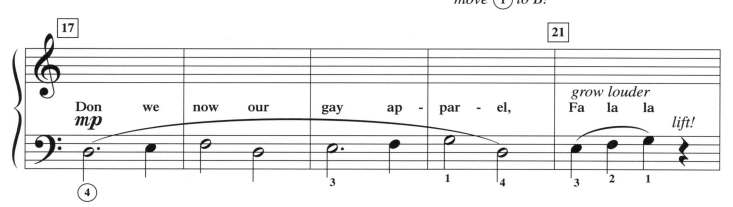

17   **21**

grow louder

Don   we   now   our   gay   ap -   par -   el,   Fa   la   la

mp   *lift!*

④   3   1   4   3   2   1

Teacher Duet: (Student plays *1 octave higher*)

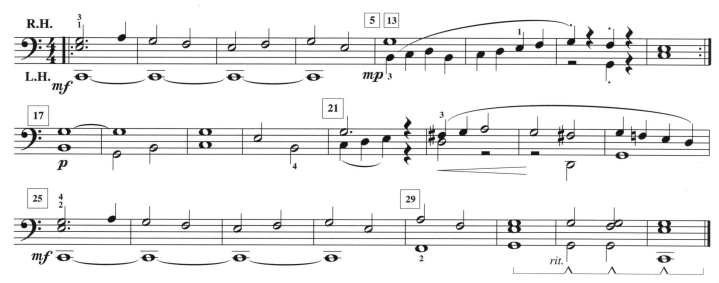

R.H. 3
      1   **5** **13**   1

mp 3

L.H. *mf*

17   **21**
                                          3

p   4

25 4
        2   **29**

mf   2   *rit.*

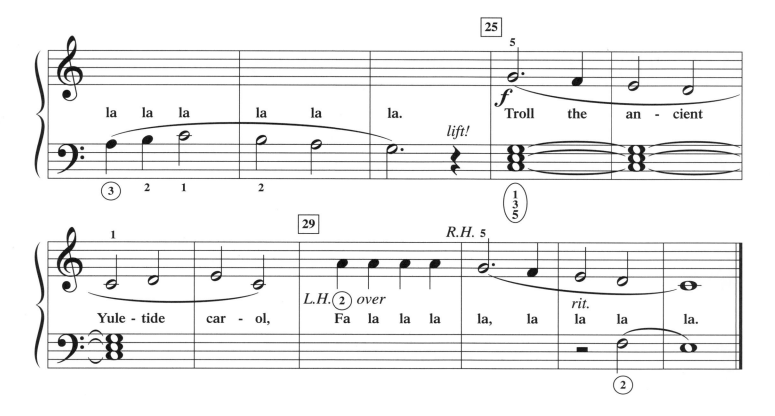

la la la   la   la   la.   *lift!*   **f** Troll   the   an - cient

Yule - tide   car - ol,   *L.H.* ② *over* Fa   la   la   la   la,   la   la   la   la.   *rit.*

Sightread one "stocking stuffer" a day while learning *Deck the Halls*.

Circle the stocking after sightreading!

F A LA LA STOCKING STUFFERS

("variations" for sightreading)

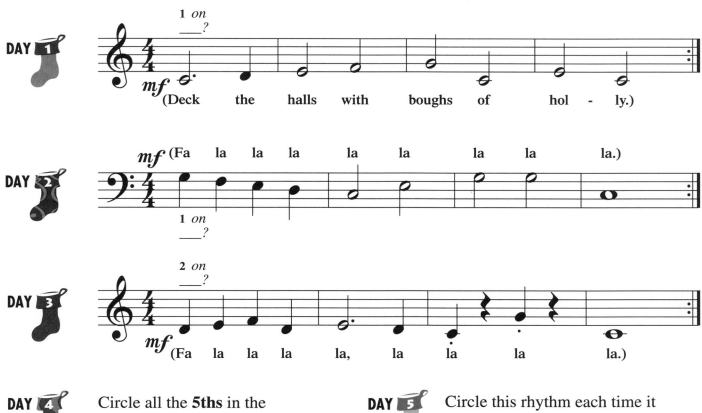

DAY 1   *1 on ___?*   **mf** (Deck   the   halls   with   boughs   of   hol - ly.)

DAY 2   **mf** (Fa   la   la   la   la   la   la   la   la.)   *1 on ___?*

DAY 3   *2 on ___?*   **mf** (Fa   la   la   la   la,   la   la   la   la.)

DAY 4   Circle all the **5ths** in the "stocking stuffers" above.

DAY 5   Circle this rhythm each time it appears in *Deck the Halls*.

♩. ♩   Hint: It occurs 6 times.

Teacher Note: Some students may wish to substitute the ♩. ♪ rhythm in measures 7, 12, and 19.

O Come, All Ye Faithful
(Adeste Fideles)

Transcribed by F. Oakeley
Wade's "Cantus Diversi"

Teacher Duet: (Student plays *1 octave higher*)

FF1138

come, let us a - dore Him, O come, let us a - dore Him, O

a little louder *big tone!*

mf *f*

come let us a - dore Him;___ Christ,___ the Lord.

(prepare)

Sightread one "stocking stuffer" a day while learning *O Come All Ye Faithful*.

Circle the stocking after sightreading!

JOYFUL STOCKING STUFFERS

("variations" for sightreading)

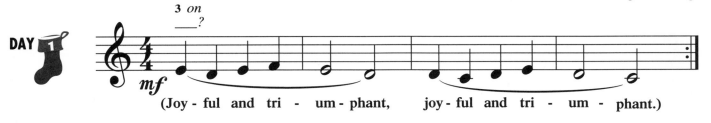

DAY 1

mf 3 on ___?

(Joy - ful and tri - um - phant, joy - ful and tri - um - phant.)

DAY 2

mf (O come ye, O come___ ye to Beth - le - hem.)

1 on ___?

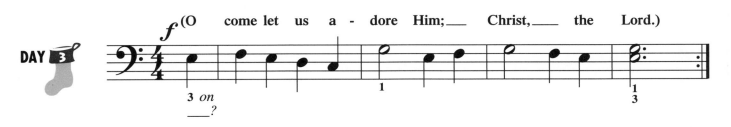

DAY 3

f (O come let us a - dore Him;___ Christ,___ the Lord.)

3 on ___?

DAY 4 Circle a C chord in the carol.

 DAY 5 Circle and label a **2nd**, a **3rd**, a **4th**, and a **5th** in the "stocking stuffers" above.

O Come, Little Children

Words and Music by
Christoph von Schmidt and J.A.P. Schulz

Gently

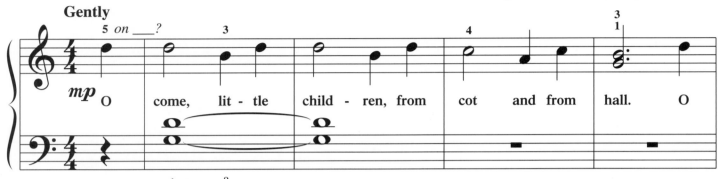

optional pedal

(optional)

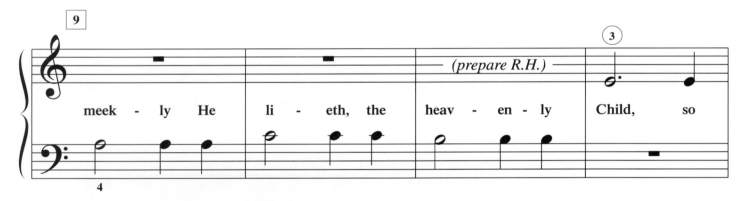

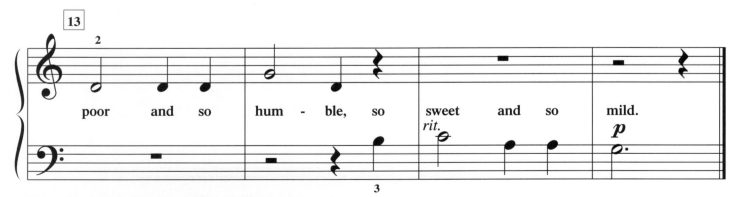

Note: Teacher duet is at the bottom of page 15.

FF1138

Sightread one "stocking stuffer" a day
while learning *O Come, Little Children.*

Circle the stocking after sightreading!

("variations" for sightreading)

DAY 1

5 *on* ___?

mp (O come, lit - tle child - ren, from cot and from hall.)

DAY 2

(There meek - ly He li - eth, the heav - en - ly Child.)

mf

3 *on* ___?

DAY 3

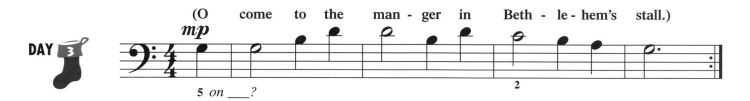

(O come to the man - ger in Beth - le - hem's stall.)

mp

5 *on* ___?

DAY 4 Write the letter names beside
each note for **Day 1.**

DAY 5 In *O Come, Little Children,* put a ✔
above each measure with this rhythm:

Hint: There are 12.

Teacher Duet for *O Come, Little Children:* (Student plays *as written.*)

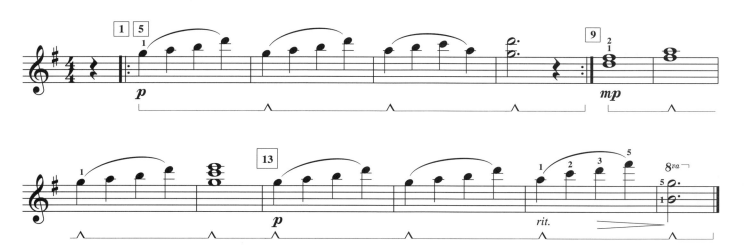

Jingle Bells

Words and Music by
J. Pierpont

Teacher Duet: (Student plays *1 octave higher*)

FF1138

For piano solo: Continue on to page 18 for more "Jingle Bell" fun!
For duet: End at measure 32.

Sightread one "stocking stuffer" a day
while learning *Jingle Bells.*

Circle the stocking after sightreading!

SLEIGHBELL STOCKING STUFFERS

("variations" for sightreading)

DAY 5 Can you sing page 17 of *Jingle Bells* without playing the piano?

Christmas Music Calendar

Complete the music calendar for each day of December.

DEC. 1 ♩ + ♩. = ___ beats	**DEC. 2** Shade the key a **3rd** higher than **C**.	**DEC. 3** Draw a **treble clef** on the ornament.	**DEC. 4** Draw a **double bar line** at the end of the sleigh.	**DEC. 5** Number Santa's fingers.
DEC. 6 Name the stars.	**DEC. 7** Draw a **bass clef** on Santa's beard.	**DEC. 8** ♩. ⌣ ♩. = ___ beats	**DEC. 9** Draw a **quarter rest** inside the wreath.	**DEC. 10** Write your favorite **time signature**.
DEC. 11 Would prancing reindeer hooves be **staccato** or **legato**? *(circle one)*	**DEC. 12** How would you rather ice skate? **legato** or **staccato**? *(circle one)*	**DEC. 13** Draw a **sharp** on the tree.	**DEC. 14** Write the dynamic mark for **loud** sleigh bells.	**DEC. 15** Write the note names for these Christmas stars.
DEC. 16 **C** up to **F** is the interval of a: **2nd 3rd 4th 5th** *(circle one)*	**DEC. 17** How many beats are in a measure for *Jingle Bells*? ___ beats	**DEC. 18** Write the dynamic mark for **soft**, fluffy snowflakes.	**DEC. 19** Draw a **flat** on the present.	**DEC. 20** **F** down to **D** is the interval of a: **2nd 3rd 4th 5th** *(circle one)*

DEC. 21 In **C** position, what note is the **tonic**? ___ the **dominant**? ___	**DEC. 22** Write the note names for these Christmas stars.	**DEC. 23** How many **E**'s (for elves) are on your piano? ___ E's

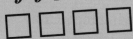

DEC. 24

Christmas Eve!
Put the dynamic marks in order, from softest to loudest.

mf f p mp

☐ ☐ ☐ ☐

DEC. 25

Christmas Day!

Play your favorite Christmas songs!